AF594812

Uncles

Morgan Brody

Creating Young Nonfiction Readers

EZ Readers lets children delve into nonfiction at beginning reading levels. Young readers are introduced to new concepts, facts, ideas, and vocabulary.

Tips for Reading Nonfiction with Beginning Readers

Talk about Nonfiction
Begin by explaining that nonfiction books give us information that is true. The book will be organized around a specific topic or idea, and we may learn new facts through reading.

Look at the Parts
Most nonfiction books have helpful features. Our *EZ Readers* include a Contents page, an index, a picture glossary, and color photographs. Share the purpose of these features with your reader.

Contents
Located at the front of a book, the Contents displays a list of the big ideas within the book and where to find them.

Index
An index is an alphabetical list of topics and the page numbers where they are found.

Picture Glossary
Located at the back of the book, a picture glossary contains key words/phrases that are related to the topic.

Photos/Charts
A lot of information can be found by "reading" the charts and photos found within nonfiction text. Help your reader learn more about the different ways information can be displayed.

With a little help and guidance about reading nonfiction, you can feel good about introducing a young reader to the world of *EZ Readers* nonfiction books.

Copyright © 2018 by Mitchell Lane Publishers. All rights reserved. No part of this book may be reproduced without written permission from the publisher.
Printed and bound in the United States of America.

Printing 1 2 3 4 5 6 7 8 9

Author: Morgan Brody
Designer: Ed Morgan
Editor: Sharon F. Dorasamy

Names/credits:
Title: Uncles / by Morgan Brody
Description: Hallandale, FL : Mitchell Lane Publishers, [2018]

Series: My Family

Library bound ISBN: 9781680202410

eBook ISBN: 9781680202427

EZ readers is an imprint of Mitchell Lane Publishers

Photo credits: Getty Images, Freepik.com

Contents

I love my uncle.

We like to play video games.

FIRST STUDENT

We like to fly
paper airplanes.

We like to arm wrestle.

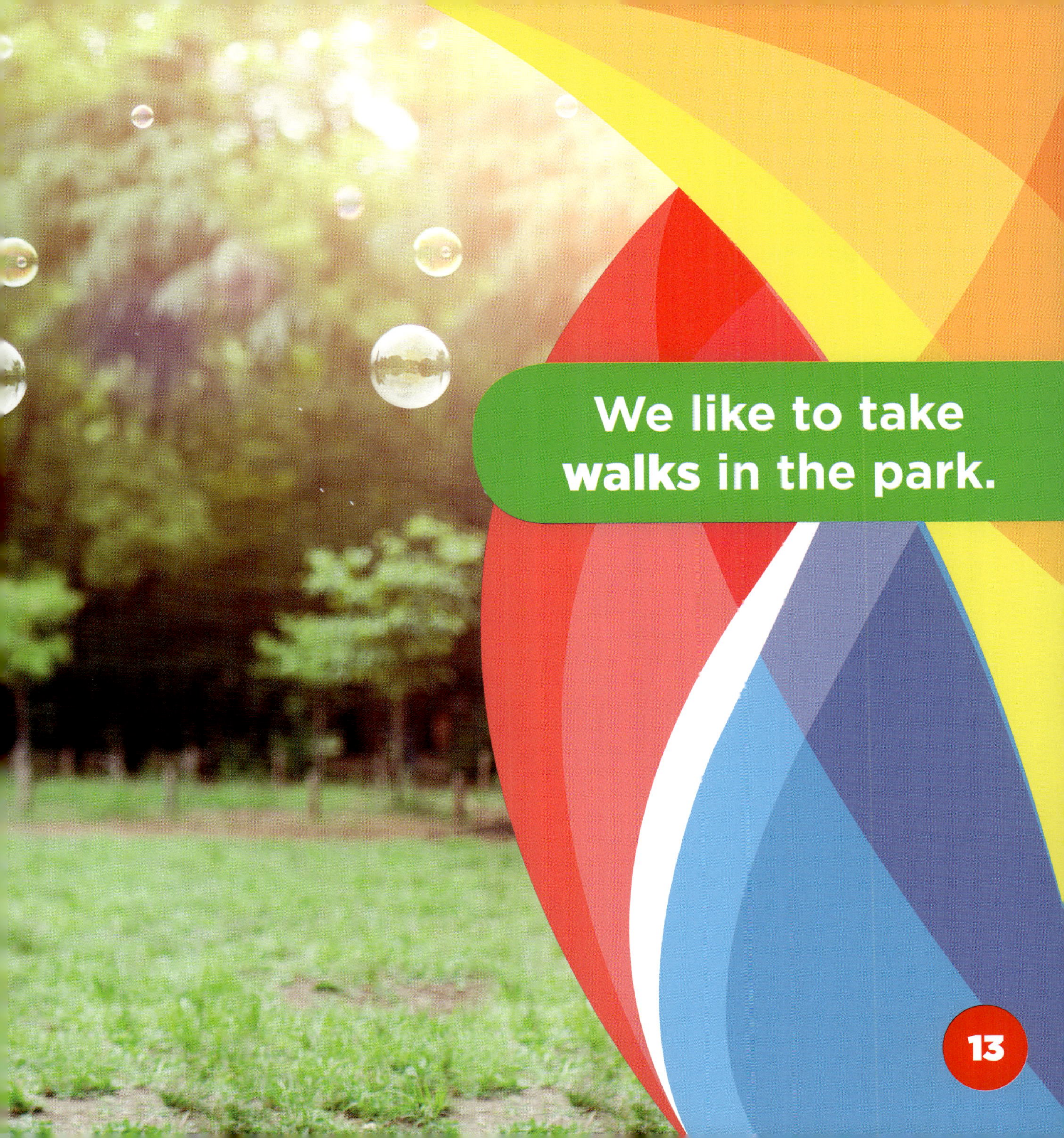

We like to take walks in the park.

We like to go to the pet shop together.

We like to wash cars together.

We like to play ball together.

My uncle is so much fun!

Picture Glossary

airplanes
A machine with wings and an engine that flies through the air

arm wrestle
A contest in which two people sit facing each other and join hands to force each other's arm down

ball
A round object that you throw, kick, or hit in a game

car
A vehicle with four wheels and an engine that is used for carrying passengers on roads

pet shop
A store that sells pets

video games
An electronic game that can be played on a TV or computer

walks
Going somewhere by walking

What are your favorite things to do with your uncle(s)?

What would you like your uncle to teach you?

What was your uncle's favorite thing to do when he was your age?

Index